Busy Bees

By Natasha Vizcarra
Illustrated by John Maynard Balinggao

Library For All Ltd.

Library For All is an Australian not for profit organisation with a mission to make knowledge accessible to all via an innovative digital library solution. Visit us at libraryforall.org

Busy Bees

This edition published 2022

Published by Library For All Ltd
Email: info@libraryforall.org
URL: libraryforall.org

This work is licensed under the Creative Commons Attribution-NonCommercial-NoDerivatives 4.0 International License. To view a copy of this license, visit http://creativecommons.org/licenses/by-nc-nd/4.0/.

Library For All gratefully acknowledges the contributions of all who made previous editions of this book possible.

This book was made possible by the generous support of Save The Children.

Original illustrations by John Maynard Balinggao

Busy Bees
Vizcarra, Natasha
ISBN: 978-1-922827-53-1
SKU02678

Busy Bees

Bees All Around

Bzzzz, bzzzz. Do you hear that? It's a bee!

You can find bees near flowers. You can find them in trees. You can find them near your home.

What Are Bees?

Bees are insects. Bees are different sizes depending on what type of bee they are, but they are small compared to humans.

Bees have wings; they have six legs; and a bottom that has black and yellow stripes.

Where Do Bees Live?

Bees live in colonies or hives. All bees in a colony work together.

Each bee has a job to do. The queen bee lays eggs. Worker bees collect food and build the honeycomb.

Worker bees also take care of the baby bees. Baby bees are called larvae.

9

What Do Bees Eat?

Bees fly from flower to flower, sipping nectar. They have a special tongue that sucks out the nectar. They store the nectar until they return to their colony.

Bees turn the nectar into honey. It is placed in honeycombs to store as food.

The honey is food for the queen, the larvae, and all the worker bees.

Bees produce two to three times more honey than they need.

That's why it's okay for people to harvest honey from bees. Honey is great on bread and fruit!

Bees also turn the honey into royal jelly. They feed this jelly to larva that will become the new queen bee.

How Bees Help Plants

When bees collect nectar, they get pollen onto their bodies. Pollen is a powdery substance that helps plants make seeds.

The bees help other plants grow by spreading pollen as they fly from flower to flower. If you love flowers, fruit, and vegetables, thank the bees!

Let's Help Bees

In the last 15 years, too many bees have disappeared. Nobody knows why. Scientists say billions of bees have left their hives and never returned.

We can help bees by planting flowers. We can help by not using harmful chemicals called pesticides on our plants.

What other ways can you think of to help bees?

Glossary

Colony: a group of bees

Hive: a place where a bee colony lives

Honeycomb: a structure made of wax that bees make to store honey and eggs

Nectar: a sugary fluid made by plants, especially flowers

You can use these questions to talk about this book with your family, friends and teachers.

What did you learn from this book?

Describe this book in one word. Funny? Scary? Colourful? Interesting?

How did this book make you feel when you finished reading it?

What was your favourite part of this book?

download our reader app
getlibraryforall.org

About the contributors

Library For All works with authors and illustrators from around the world to develop diverse, relevant, high quality stories for young readers. Visit libraryforall.org for the latest news on writers' workshop events, submission guidelines and other creative opportunities.

Did you enjoy this book?

We have hundreds more expertly curated original stories to choose from.

We work in partnership with authors, educators, cultural advisors, governments and NGOs to bring the joy of reading to children everywhere.

Did you know?

We create global impact in these fields by embracing the United Nations Sustainable Development Goals.

libraryforall.org

www.ingramcontent.com/pod-product-compliance
Lightning Source LLC
Chambersburg PA
CBHW040315050426
42452CB00018B/2847